INSIGHTS

ENERGY

ROBIN KERROD

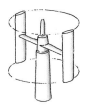

INSIGHTS

ENERGY

ROBIN KERROD

Oxford University Press

A QUARTO BOOK
Published by
Oxford University Press, Walton Street, Oxford, OX2 6DP
Oxford New York Toronto Delhi Bombay Calcutta Madras Karachi
Petaling Jaya Singapore Hong Kong Tokyo Nairobi Dar Es Salaam Cape Town

and associated companies in Berlin Ibadan

Oxford is a trade mark of Oxford University Press

A catalogue record for this book is available from the British Library.

ISBN 0 19 910055 1

This book was designed and produced by
Quarto Children's Books Ltd
1 Carpenters Mews North Road London N7 9EF

Art Director Nick Buzzard
Managing Editor Christine Hatt

Editor Maggi McCormick
Designer Steven Wilson
Illustrators Janos Marffy, Paul Richardson, Guy Smith Mainline Design
Picture Researcher Liz Eddison

The Publishers would like to thank the following for their help in the
preparation of this book: Karen Ball.

Picture Acknowledgements
Quarto Publishing would like to thank the following for supplying photographs
and for permission to reproduce copyright material. While every effort has
been made to trace and acknowledge all copyright holders, we would like to
apologize should any omissions have been made.

Australian Tourist Board, page 28ar. Cern Photography, page 41bl. Colorific,
pages 18bl, 18br, 29bl, 36al, 36c. Japanese Tourist Board, page 19br. Jet
Joint Undertaking, page 51br. Robin Kerrod, pages 14cl, 23ar, 34bl, 37cr,
39al. Sci Pix, pages 11al, 15bl, 30br, 35ar, 41al, 41cl. Spacecharts, pages
12ar, 14ar, 26cr, 39br, 43ac. Telegraph Colour Library UK, pages 10bl, 11bl,
13br (inside flap), 17cl, 17a, 18cr, 19cl, 20br, 21br, 22cl, 25cl, 27cl, 27b, 27ar,
29c (inside flap), 30bl, 31bl, 33al, 33br, 34cr, 37ar, 38c, 43bl, 44cr, 45ar,
46br, 47br, 48bl, 49c, 49ar, 50c, 51al. Trip, pages 10cr, 16al (inside flap),
17br, 25ar, 30cr, 30c, 42cl, 51ar. Flora Torrance, page 45al. Tony Waltham,
page 29a. Jon Woodhouse, page 13al.
Key: a = above, b = below, l = left, r = right, c = centre

Front jacket photographs supplied by: Telegraph Colour Library UK –
above left and bottom centre, Colorific – bottom left.
Back jacket photograph supplied by: Robin Kerrod.

Typeset by Central Southern Typesetters, Eastbourne, East Sussex
Manufactured in Singapore by Eray Scan Pte Ltd
Printed in Singapore by Star Standard Industries (Pte) Ltd

CONTENTS

ENERGY ALL AROUND

To pedal our bikes, heat our homes, turn on the lights, and sail our boats, we need energy. To pedal our bikes, we use the energy stored in our muscles. To heat our homes, we use the energy from burning fuels. To turn on the lights, we use electricity. To sail our boats, we use the energy blowing in the wind. Muscle power, heat, electricity, and wind power are just four of the many kinds of energy we come across in the world about us.

Any objects that have energy, no matter what form it takes, have something in common. Their energy gives them the ability to do work. Energy stored in your arm muscles is ready to throw a ball. Energy stored in a battery is ready to turn the tape in a cassette recorder. Energy stored in petrol is ready to power a car engine and turn the wheels. As you see, energy is often connected with movement.

▼ **Balancing boulder**
This collection of rocks, in Australia's Northern Territory, is called the Devil's Marbles. The boulder precariously balanced on top has considerable potential energy, which it would release as kinetic energy if it fell.

◄ **Speed skater**
Bursting with energy, a roller skater speeds over the ground. He is harnessing chemical energy in his body, which causes his leg muscles to contract and produce the movement that propels him.

► **Light at night**
As the Sun goes down, the lights go on in New York City skyscrapers. At the flick of a switch, electrical energy is converted to light as it surges through millions of bulbs, lamps, and tubes.

Everything has energy of one kind or another. An apple on a tree has energy. When it is ripe, it falls. On the tree it has potential energy, or energy because of its position. When it falls, it starts losing its potential energy. At the same time it starts gaining the energy of movement, or kinetic energy.

Everything that is moving has kinetic energy, and the faster something is moving, the more kinetic energy it has. You can knock down a skittle with a fast ball much more easily than you can with a slow one, because the fast ball contains much more energy.

Heat, light, and sound

Heat is perhaps the most familiar form of energy. But it is in fact a form of kinetic energy. An object has heat energy because of the movement of the particles that make it up. In a similar way sound is a kind of kinetic energy, because it depends on the movement of the particles that make up the air.

▼ Hot stuff

A crucible is removed from the very hot furnace in which it has been baked. It has a very high temperature and possesses a lot of energy, which it gives off as heat that we can feel and light that we can see.

Heat also travels to the Earth from the Sun in the form of rays, which are called radiant energy. Light, X-rays, and radio waves are also forms of radiant energy.

Energy changes

When we strike a match, the energy stored in the wood is released and appears as light and heat. In other words, an energy change has taken place. Energy was stored in the wood in the form of chemical energy. Burning changed the chemical energy into heat energy and light energy.

Energy is also stored in a torch battery in the form of chemical energy. When you switch on the torch, some of this chemical energy is converted to electrical energy. This travels into the coil filament

▶ Solar electric
Thousands of little solar cells made of silicon chips cover the body of this GOES (Geostationary Operational Environmental Satellite). Each cell produces a tiny electric current when sunlight hits it. When the currents are combined, all the weather satellite's instruments are able to work.

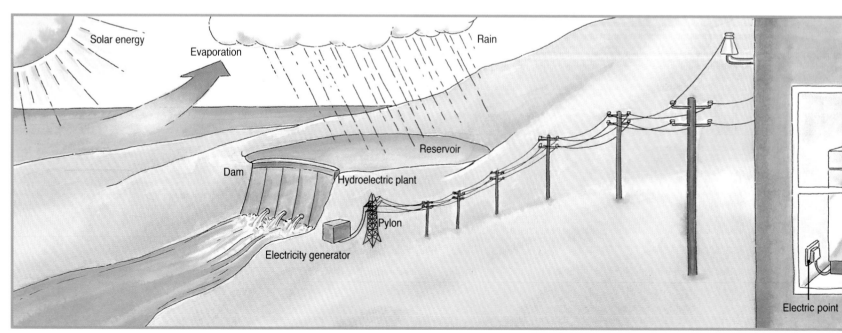

Solar energy

Evaporation

Rain

Reservoir

Dam

Hydroelectric plant

Pylon

Electricity generator

Electric point

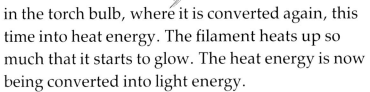

in the torch bulb, where it is converted again, this time into heat energy. The filament heats up so much that it starts to glow. The heat energy is now being converted into light energy.

Changes in energy go on all the time in our world. But if you measured accurately the amount of energy before and the amount of energy after all the changes, you would find that they were the same. This fact obeys a basic law of nature known as the conservation of energy: energy can neither be created nor destroyed, only changed to other forms.

▲ The big bang

An apartment block crumbles and collapses when explosives are detonated at its base. The explosion gives out enormous energy as shock waves. Their energy blasts away the main supports of the building. Then gravity takes over, and the upper floors come tumbling down.

CYCLING THE ENERGY

Energy changes take place all around us all the time. When you plug in a washing machine, electrical energy is converted to heat energy to heat the water and mechanical energy to spin the drum. But this is only part of the energy conversion story. In this case, the story begins with the Sun evaporating water from the sea.

WHO'S WATT?

The Scottish engineer James Watt (1736–1819) is often called the 'father of the steam engine'. A favourite story about Watt tells how his ideas about steam power were triggered off by seeing steam spurt from a boiling kettle and lift its lid.

Watt did not invent the steam engine, but he improved it in the 1770s. Our unit of power, the watt, is named after him.

▼ A box of tricks

This wooden box is full of energy, in more ways than one. When it rests on a table, it has potential energy. If it is accidentally nudged off the edge of the table, it will fall. The box also contains chemical energy locked in the wood it is made of. If the box were set alight, it would burn. This energy would then be released as heat and light. There might well be something else energetic inside the box. Let's undo the catch.

SUN POWER

I n one way or another the Sun provides most of the energy on Earth. Day after day it pours out heat and light that keep our world warm and bright. It gives plants the energy they need to grow and make food. Also, the fuels we burn are the remains of living things that trapped the Sun's energy millions of years ago. We can think of them as stored sunlight.

▲ Solar flare
A gigantic tongue of flame called a solar flare shoots high above the surface of the Sun. When solar flares occur, streams of particles flow into space like a gusting wind. When this solar wind reaches the Earth, it disrupts radio communications.

◄ Pelican at sunset
The Sun becomes dimmer as it sets because its light is passing through the thickest part of the atmosphere.

We get most of our energy from the Sun, but where does the Sun get its energy?

Astronomers tell us that the Sun has been shining the way it does today for about 5,000 million years. So it cannot be burning coal or natural gas or any other ordinary fuel, or it would have fizzled out long ago.

Clearly, the Sun must have quite a different method of producing energy, and we now know what this method is. It is a process called nuclear fusion, because it involves the fusion (joining together) of the nuclei (centres) of hydrogen atoms.

When this happens, in the centre of the Sun, enormous amounts of energy are given out, and the temperature reaches 15,000,000°C (27,000,000°F) or more. The energy travels to the outer surface of the Sun and is radiated into space as heat, light, and other radiation. Eight-and-a-half minutes after leaving the Sun, this radiation reaches the Earth.

Our neighbourhood star

Nuclear fusion is also the process that keeps the stars shining. This is not so surprising because the Sun is in fact just another star. It appears very much

◄ The stormy Sun

The surface of the Sun is a seething mass of searing hot gas at a temperature of about 5,500°C (10,000°F). It is in constant turmoil, with great tongues of flame and fiery fountains leaping thousands of kilometres high.

▼ Imitating the Sun

This flash of light was produced when a powerful laser machine brought about fusion in a tiny speck of nuclear fuel. Bombarding the fuel with lasers is one way in which scientists try to imitate the energy-making process that goes on in the Sun.

Hydrogen nucleus

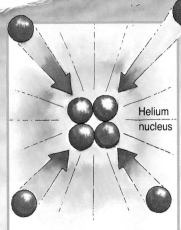

Helium nucleus

NUCLEAR FUSION

In the heart of the Sun, hydrogen atoms combine, or fuse together, to form helium atoms. This nuclear fusion process produces the enormous energy that makes the Sun shine.

LIVING IN A GREENHOUSE

The Earth's atmosphere helps keep us warm at night by trapping some of the Sun's daytime heat. In other words, it acts like a kind of greenhouse.

Unfortunately, in recent years the atmosphere has been trapping more and more of the Sun's heat. This is happening largely because increasing amounts of carbon dioxide are getting into the air from car exhausts and chimneys.

As a result, our world is gradually getting warmer. But if it gets too warm, our weather will change, probably for the worse.

Atmosphere

Earth

Sun's energy

Trapped heat

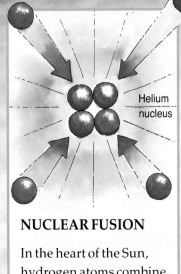

88051915

200 MICRONS

SHIVA FIRST 20 BEAM SHOT
26 TH / 95 PS
7.5 X 10**9 NEUTRONS
2 KEV X-RAYS

bigger and brighter than the other stars simply because it is very much closer to Earth. It lies only 150 million kilometres (93 million miles) away. This may not seem close, but it is when compared with the distance to all the other stars. Even the nearest star, Proxima Centauri, lies more than 40 million million kilometres (25 million million miles) away!

The Sun is not a very big star, measuring about 1,400,000 kilometres (865,000 miles) across. Some stars are hundreds of times bigger. If they were as close to Earth as the Sun is, the Earth would be a burnt-out cinder of a planet.

PHOTOSYNTHESIS

In photosynthesis, a plant makes its sugary food from water it takes in through its roots and from carbon dioxide it takes in from the air. The energy for the process comes from sunlight.

Sunlight

Carbon dioxide

Water

Sugar

Oxygen

▼ **Grazing and snoozing**
On the savannah of East Africa, antelope graze peacefully on the coarse grass. Because their food does not contain much energy, they spend most of their lives eating. Meanwhile, the lion sleeps, as he often does during the day.

ENERGY FOR LIFE

All living things, plants and animals alike, need a constant supply of energy to stay alive. Plants take in energy from the Sun to make food. They use some of this food to give them energy to grow, and store the rest. Animals need energy not only to grow but also to move about. Unlike plants, they cannot make their own food. They have to get their energy by eating food that plants have made, or by eating other animals that eat plants.

Plants make their food from water and carbon dioxide gas. They combine these simple ingredients to make sugars and starches, which are chemical compounds called carbohydrates. Foodmaking takes place in the leaves. Water enters a plant through its roots and travels to the leaves through the plant tissues. Carbon dioxide is taken in from the air, entering the leaves through minute holes, or pores, called stomata.

A plant can only make food in the light, because sunlight is needed to provide the energy for the foodmaking. That is why the process is called photosynthesis ('making with light'). The Sun's

▶ Busy bee

A bee sips the sweet-tasting nectar of a flower. Later it will return to the hive and use the nectar it has gathered to help build the honeycomb and feed the bee larvae (young). Bees, and many other insects, play another vital role in nature. They spread pollen from one flower to another. This makes it possible for the plants to reproduce.

FOOD FOR LIFE

Like all living things, human beings need to take in food to stay alive. We can eat many different kinds of food, both animal and vegetable. We are omnivores, a word that means 'eat all'.

Milk is one of the best foods, because it contains most of the essential substances that our bodies need: carbohydrates which give us energy, proteins which build up our bodies, and vitamins which keep us healthy.

energy is captured by the green substance in the leaves, a pigment called chlorophyll.

Living and breathing

Photosynthesis produces not only sugar, but also oxygen, which is given off into the atmosphere. Plants therefore play a vital part in our world, not only by making food but also by keeping it supplied with oxygen, which all living creatures must breathe to stay alive. Breathing, or respiration, is part of the process that provides living things with the energy they need. They get their energy by 'burning' foods such as carbohydrates in the body cells. For burning to take place, the cells must be provided with oxygen. Breathing supplies this oxygen.

Different animals breathe in different ways. Humans and many other animals breathe through their lungs. But fish breathe through their gills, and insects breathe through tiny tubes called spiracles.

▼ Plant parasites

Not all plants make their own food by photosynthesis. Fungi, for example, get their food from other plants. They are parasites. Dead and dying trees are a favourite target for them. Because they do not need light to make their food, fungi grow quite happily in the dark.

HOT AND COLD

▼ **Fire in the forest**
When a forest is very dry, it catches fire easily. In a strong wind, a forest fire can spread faster than you are able to run and can cause untold destruction. Burning is a chemical process called oxidation, in which chemicals in the wood combine with oxygen in the air. This process releases energy as heat, which we can feel, and as light, which we can see as flames.

Heat is one of the most common forms of energy, and one that we can feel. The Sun's heat warms our world and makes it able to support an enormous variety of life. The level of heat in the atmosphere is the main factor that affects our weather. We use the heat given out by burning fuels to drive the engines and turbines that power our cars, aircraft, and rockets. We also use another kind of heat engine, a refrigerator, to remove heat from things or make them colder.

We can feel the heat and we can feel the cold, which is simply a lack of heat. But what exactly is heat? To answer that question, we must look at the tiny particles – the atoms and molecules – that make up matter.

If we could see these particles, we would find that they are always moving. In solids they just vibrate, but in liquids and gases they are able to move more freely. We would find that they move faster in a hot substance than they do in a cold one, so we can say that heat is a property that depends on the energy of movement, that is the kinetic energy, of its particles.

FROM TROPICS TO TUNDRA

Different parts of the world receive different amounts of heat from the Sun. This makes them have different climates. The Tropics region around the Equator has the hottest climate. Regions near the North and South Poles are the coldest.

Cold-blooded creatures such as lizards (left) like tropical climates. They need to soak up the Sun's heat to warm up their blood. In the snow-bound north, warm-blooded deer (right) remain active in temperatures below freezing because their blood temperature is controlled inside their bodies.

▼ The frozen north

A sparkling icy scene in the far north of Canada inside the Arctic Circle. There, the temperature stays below freezing for much of the year. During the long winter it can plummet to below −50°C (−60°F). But the lowest temperatures on Earth occur on the other side of the world, in Antarctica, where temperatures approaching −90°C (−130°F) have been recorded.

KEEPING COOL

In a refrigerator, a liquid called a refrigerant is first evaporated (turned to gas), then condensed (turned back to liquid). As it evaporates inside coils in the refrigerator, it takes in heat. As it does this, it cools the food.

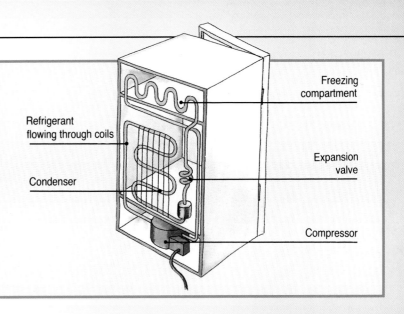

Freezing compartment

Refrigerant flowing through coils

Condenser

Expansion valve

Compressor

SUPERCOLD AND SUPERCONDUCTORS

If we lower the temperature enough, we can make the very air we breathe condense, or turn into a liquid. This happens at a temperature of about −250°C (−420°F). Helium gas does not turn into a liquid until about −270°C (−455°F).

When things are cooled this way, strange things happen. If we put electric current into a wire, it flows with no resistance. The wire becomes what we call a superconductor.

Using this principle, we can make superconducting magnets that use hardly any electricity. These are used in trains like the one below, which glide above the track, supported by magnetism. They are called maglev (magnetically levitated) trains.

Degrees of heat

We describe how hot or cold something is by its temperature, and measure this with a thermometer (meaning 'heat-measurer').

Temperature is measured in units called degrees. There are two common temperature scales. The Celsius scale uses degrees Celsius (°C), and is named after Anders Celsius, the Swedish chemist who suggested it. On this scale water freezes at 0 degrees and boils at 100 degrees. The Fahrenheit scale uses degrees Fahrenheit (°F), and is named

Thermometer scale (left side)

°F | °C
212 — 200 — 100 — Water boils
173.3 — 80 / 78.5 — Alcohol boils
150 — 60
98.4 — 100 — 40 / 36.9 — Normal blood temperature
70 — 21 / 20 — Average room temperature
50
32 — 0 — Water freezes
3.9 — 0 — −15.6 — Anti-freeze freezes
−20
−40
−50
−60
−100
−112 — −80 — Lowest recorded temperature

after a German physicist, Gabriel Daniel Fahrenheit. On this scale the freezing point of water is 32 degrees and the boiling point is 212 degrees. The temperature of our world varies widely. It is lowest at the Poles, where temperatures can drop below −80°C (−112°F). It is highest in desert regions, where temperatures can reach more than 50°C (122°F). Human beings find it most pleasant to live in places with a temperature of about 20–25°C (68–77°F).

Expanding and contracting

The ordinary outdoor thermometer we use is a glass tube containing a liquid, such as mercury (silver-coloured) or coloured alcohol (red). When the weather gets warmer, the column of liquid gets longer. And when it gets colder, the column gets shorter. This happens because substances expand (get bigger) when they are heated, and contract (get smaller) when they are cooled. Liquids expand more than solids, but not as much as gases.

◀ **Temperature levels**
An ordinary thermometer is a sealed glass tube containing a liquid. The level of the liquid rises when the temperature goes up and falls when the temperature goes down. Marked on this thermometer are some familiar temperatures given in both degrees Celsius and Fahrenheit.

▶ **Suited for firefighting**
Clad in shiny asbestos suits, firefighters walk right up to the flames. The asbestos stops the heat from passing through because it is a very good heat insulator.

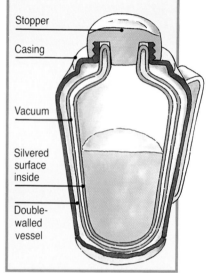

KEEP IT HOT

If we want to keep a hot drink hot, we keep it in a vacuum flask. This glass vessel has a double wall with an insulating vacuum in between. The inside walls are silvered to reflect the heat.

Stopper
Casing
Vacuum
Silvered surface inside
Double-walled vessel

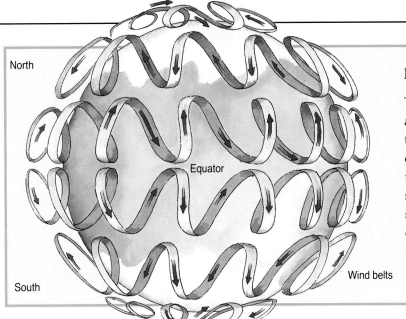

North

Equator

South

Wind belts

Temperature differences around the world give rise to the winds. If the Earth did not turn, winds would tend to blow in a north-south direction. But the spinning of the Earth deflects the winds so that they blow east or west.

GOOD CONDUCT

If you put butter on a wooden pencil and on plastic and metal spoons and place them in hot water, the butter on the metal spoon melts first: metal is a good conductor. The butter on the wood melts last: wood is a poor conductor, and so a good insulator.

Plastic

Wood

Metal

Heat on the move

If you dip the end of a cold metal spoon into hot water, the handle of the spoon soon gets hot. The particles in the water pass on heat to the particles in the end of the spoon. They pass on heat to their neighbours, and the heat travels along the spoon. This process of passing on heat is called conduction and is one of three main ways in which heat travels.

Another way is by convection. This is the method by which a radiator heats a room. The air near the radiator gets hot and expands. As it expands, it becomes lighter than the air around it and floats upwards. Colder, heavier air takes its place and expands and rises in turn. In this way a current of air begins circulating around the room. Similar convection currents in the atmosphere give rise to winds.

The third main way in which heat can travel is by radiation. The heat from the Sun travels to Earth in this way through the emptiness of space. This is because it takes the form of heat rays, which belong to the same family of rays as light (see pages 26–27). Rays from the Sun are called infrared rays, but it is not only the Sun that gives off heat rays. Any hot body does, even the human body!

▼ **Heat mapping**
Every object gives out heat rays to a lesser or greater extent. Our bodies do, too. Instruments can pick up these rays and show how the temperature varies slightly all over the body.

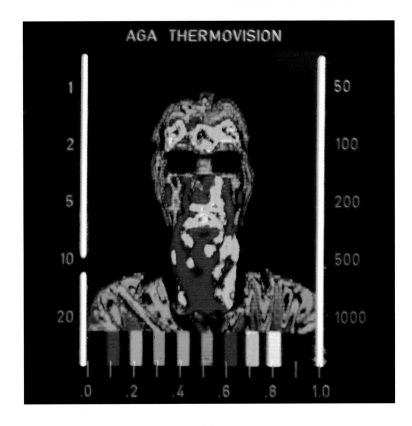

AGA THERMOVISION

ELECTRICITY AND MAGNETISM

Electricity is without doubt our most useful form of energy, available at the flick of a switch. It lights our bulbs, heats our cookers, and powers all kinds of devices and machines, from video recorders to vacuum cleaners, lasers to locomotives. Electricity is closely related to magnetism because wires become magnetic when they carry electric current.

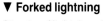

▼ Forked lightning
Streaks of lightning stab the evening sky in Arizona, USA. They show the path of high-voltage electricity from the thunderclouds to the ground. Electrical 'pressures' of millions of volts are involved.

FRANKLIN'S KITE

In the 1700s an American scientist named Benjamin Franklin carried out a dangerous experiment. He flew a kite up into a thundercloud to prove that lightning was a form of electricity. It is, and it was a miracle that Franklin was not struck by the lightning and killed. But he survived and became a great politician and one of the authors of the US Constitution.

The word electricity comes from a Greek word meaning 'amber'. Amber is a substance like the rosin that comes from pine trees. When you rub it, it attracts fluff, bits of paper, and other light objects. The same thing happens to a plastic comb when you comb your hair vigorously. That becomes attractive too.

By rubbing and combing, you give amber and plastic an electric attraction, or charge. But it is not the ordinary kind of electricity, which flows in wires. It is a form we call static electricity because it tends to stay where it is. Only when something has a very high electric charge does the electricity move. Then it suddenly jumps and even becomes visible as an electric spark. This sometimes happens in the clouds, and we see the spark as lightning.

Electricity under pressure

Static electricity is not as useful as ordinary, flowing electricity. This is the kind that flows in metal

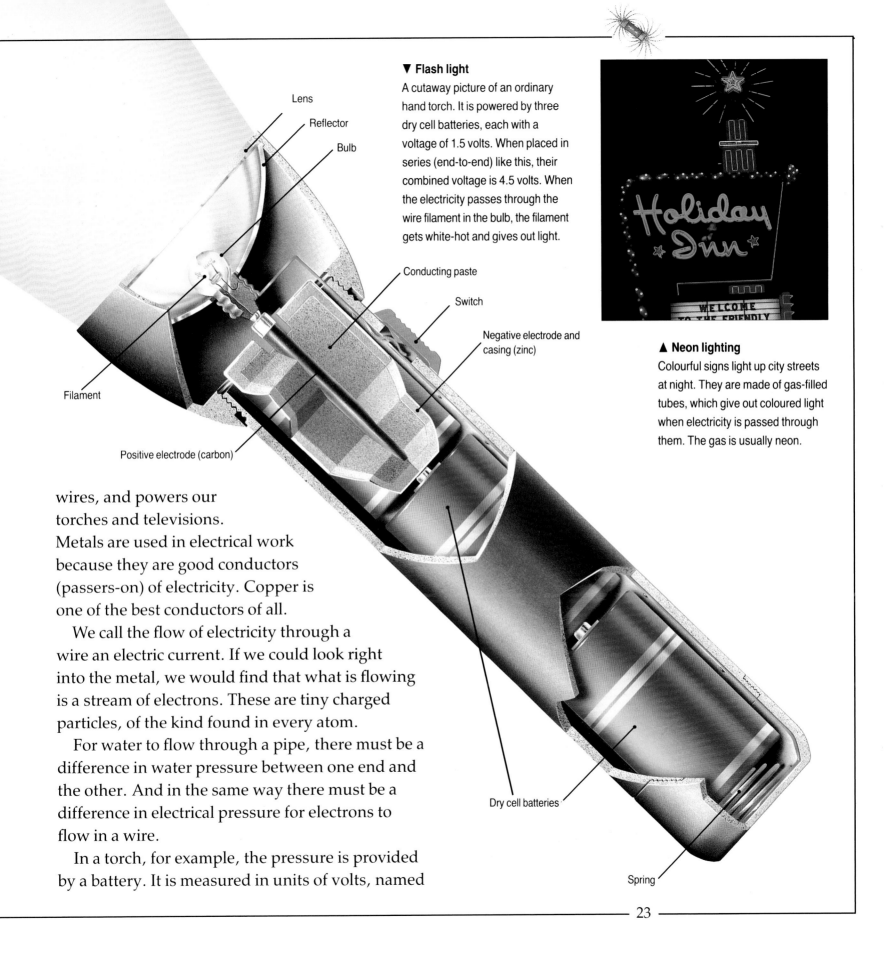

Lens

Reflector

Bulb

Filament

Positive electrode (carbon)

Conducting paste

Switch

Negative electrode and casing (zinc)

Dry cell batteries

Spring

▼ **Flash light**
A cutaway picture of an ordinary hand torch. It is powered by three dry cell batteries, each with a voltage of 1.5 volts. When placed in series (end-to-end) like this, their combined voltage is 4.5 volts. When the electricity passes through the wire filament in the bulb, the filament gets white-hot and gives out light.

▲ **Neon lighting**
Colourful signs light up city streets at night. They are made of gas-filled tubes, which give out coloured light when electricity is passed through them. The gas is usually neon.

wires, and powers our torches and televisions. Metals are used in electrical work because they are good conductors (passers-on) of electricity. Copper is one of the best conductors of all.

We call the flow of electricity through a wire an electric current. If we could look right into the metal, we would find that what is flowing is a stream of electrons. These are tiny charged particles, of the kind found in every atom.

For water to flow through a pipe, there must be a difference in water pressure between one end and the other. And in the same way there must be a difference in electrical pressure for electrons to flow in a wire.

In a torch, for example, the pressure is provided by a battery. It is measured in units of volts, named

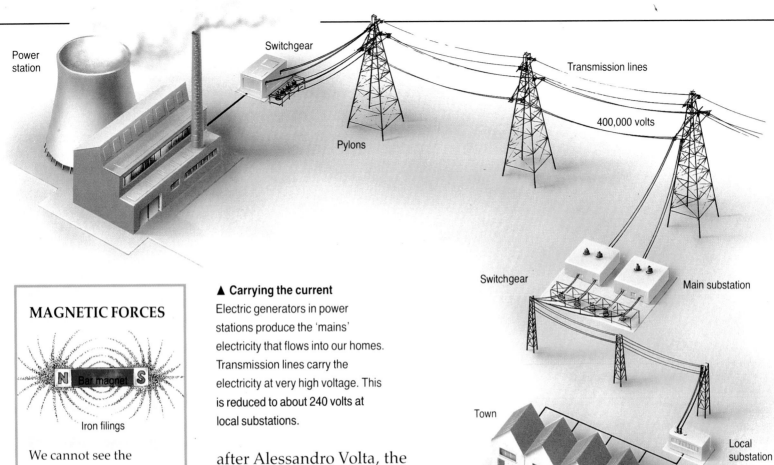

Power station

Switchgear

Transmission lines

Pylons

400,000 volts

Switchgear

Main substation

Town

240 volts

Local substation

▲ Carrying the current

Electric generators in power stations produce the 'mains' electricity that flows into our homes. Transmission lines carry the electricity at very high voltage. This is reduced to about 240 volts at local substations.

MAGNETIC FORCES

N Bar magnet S

Iron filings

We cannot see the magnetic forces around a magnet, but we can see their effects if we sprinkle some iron filings around it. The filings arrange themselves in curved lines (above), which show the direction of the magnetic forces.

Most magnetism in a magnet is concentrated at the ends, or poles, which we call north and south. Two unlike poles will attract each other. Two like poles will repel each other.

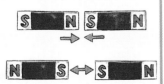

after Alessandro Volta, the Italian physicist who invented the battery. In the home, however, electrical pressure is provided by the mains. This carries electricity produced by machines called generators, which are a long distance away.

Magnets and compasses

Amber and plastic can attract things when they are rubbed. But some metals can attract things naturally. We call them magnets. Among common metals, only iron has this property. But it can only attract iron and a few metals like it.

A strange thing happens if you hang a magnet on a thread. It always comes to rest pointing north-south. This is the principle behind the compass, which helps us find direction. A magnet lines up in this way because the Earth itself behaves like a huge magnet.

ELECTRIC MOTOR

When electric current is passed through a coil, the coil becomes a kind of magnet. If this coil is placed between the poles of another magnet, the coil magnet is attracted on one side and repelled on the other side by the other magnet. This makes it turn.

24

▼ Magnetic lights

Sometimes charged particles trapped by the Earth's magnetic field pour down into the atmosphere. As they hit particles of air, they give out flashes of light, which we see as the aurora, shimmering curtains of coloured light.

MAGNETIC RINGS

When you push the button of an electric bell, current from a battery flows through an electromagnet. This becomes magnetic and attracts a clapper, which hits the bell and makes it ring.

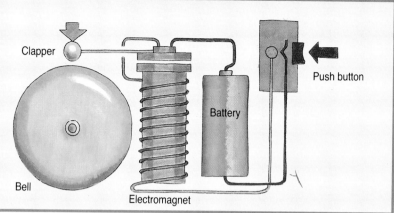

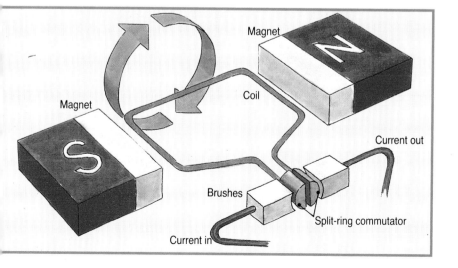

▶ Any old iron

At a scrapyard a mobile crane uses an electromagnet to pick up iron scrap. The electromagnet is a disc of soft iron containing coils of wire. When electric current is passed through the coils, the disc becomes a powerful magnet.

Coils and current

When electric current passes through a wire, it makes the wire slightly magnetic. If the wire is wound into a coil, the coil turns into a strong magnet, called an electromagnet. But it stays magnetic only as long as the current is flowing. Powerful electromagnets are widely used in industry for lifting heavy objects, while small ones are used in devices like electric bells.

Electromagnetic coils also form essential parts of the electric motors in machines like electric drills and toy trains. The pushing and pulling between magnetized coils carrying electric current produces movement. The reverse can also happen: movement between coils can produce electric current. This is the principle behind electric generators, the huge machines that produce our mains electricity.

RADIATION

T he Sun gives out energy in the form of light rays we can see and heat rays we can feel. But it also pours out energy in the form of many other kinds of rays that we cannot see or feel. They include gamma rays, X-rays, and radio waves. All these rays are different kinds of electromagnetic radiation. They take the form of electric and magnetic ripples, or waves, that all travel through space and the air at the speed of light.

The main difference between the various kinds of electromagnetic wave is that they have different wavelengths. The length of a wave is the distance between one crest (high point) and the next.

Gamma rays have the shortest wavelength: just a few million-millionths of a metre! Then, in order of increasing wavelength, come X-rays, ultraviolet rays, visible light from violet to red, infrared rays, microwaves, and finally radio waves. The longest radio waves have a wavelength of several kilometres.

Windows in the atmosphere

Only some of the electromagnetic waves the Sun gives out reach us on Earth. The atmosphere blocks the rest. It lets through only visible light, a little

▼ **Outer space radio**
The Sun, the stars, and the galaxies give out part of their energy as radio waves. Astronomers pick up heavenly radio waves with radio telescopes, and process the signals to produce photographs like this one of a distant galaxy.

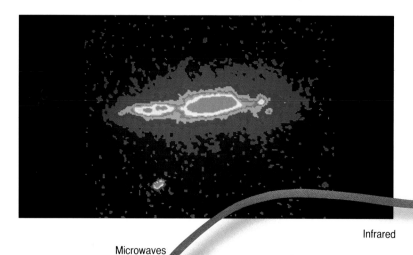

Infrared

Microwaves

Radar

Radio

▲ **Changing waves**
This wave shows how the wavelength of electromagnetic radiation varies. This end represents the long waves, such as radio waves, which measure several kilometres.

AT THE SPEED OF LIGHT

Electromagnetic rays have a regular motion, rippling up and down like an ocean wave. Each kind of ray has a typical width, or wavelength. Each travels at the same speed, the speed of light. In a vacuum this is nearly 300,000 km (186,000 miles) per second, the fastest speed possible in the Universe.

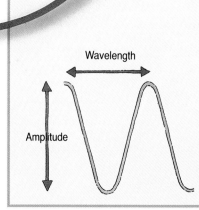

Wavelength

Amplitude

ultraviolet and infrared, and radio waves. It blocks out all gamma rays and X-rays and most ultraviolet. It is fortunate for us that it does, because these rays would harm us if they reached us all the time.

The Sun is not the only source of electromagnetic waves. We can also produce them artificially on Earth, and have found many uses for them. We use X-rays to look inside our bodies, microwaves for radar and cooking, and radio waves for communications.

Gamma ray

X-ray

Ultraviolet

Visible

▲ Rainbow colours
Light is electromagnetic radiation that we can see. It ranges in wavelength between 4 (violet light) and 7 (red light) ten-millionths of a metre (16–27 millionths of an inch).

▶ Seeing inside
Doctors check a patient's X-ray photographs. X-rays pass readily through flesh, but not so easily through bones, which therefore show up plainly on the photographs.

OZONE PROTECTION

Life on Earth would be at risk if we were exposed to all the ultraviolet radiation from the Sun. Fortunately, much of it is absorbed by a layer of ozone gas high in the atmosphere. However, substances called CFCs (chlorofluorocarbons), which are used in refrigerators and aerosol sprays, are eating into this layer, allowing more radiation through.

Ultraviolet light

Ozone layer

Earth

▲ Light industry
Laser light is used in industry to cut steel very accurately and cleanly.

▶ Burning rays
Be careful not to stay too long in strong sunlight. Ultraviolet rays can burn the body.

FOSSIL FUELS

Most of the energy we use in the modern world comes from burning coal, oil, and natural gas. We obtain these fuels by mining and drilling underground. We call them fossil fuels because they are the remains of organisms that lived on the Earth millions of years ago. Coal is the fossilized remains of huge, tree-like plants. Oil and gas are the remains of minute sea creatures and plants. Oil is by far the most important source of energy today. The world uses 4 million litres (about 900,000 gallons) of it every minute of every day in the form of petrol, diesel oil, jet fuel, and other products.

Most of our coal started forming about 300 million years ago during a time in the Earth's history we

▲ Layers of coal
A vast mountain of coal being dug at an opencast mine in Australia. The coal is excavated in a series of deeper and deeper terraces. Holes are drilled at the upper levels, and then the coal 'cliffs' are brought down by explosives. At the lower levels, power loaders then move in to load the broken-up coal onto trucks which remove it from the mine.

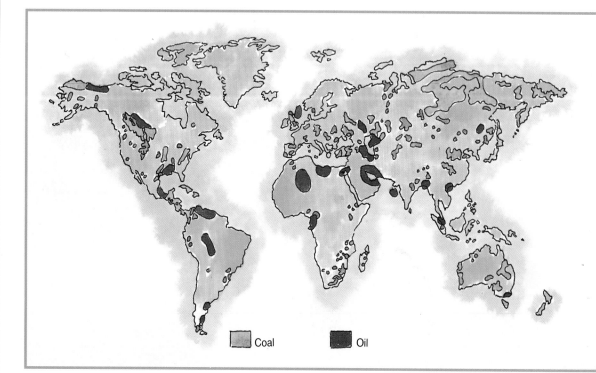

Coal ▢   Oil ■

COAL AND OIL DEPOSITS

Coal and oil are found only in certain places in the world, where conditions 300 million years ago were suitable for fossil fuel formation. Coal is found more widely than oil. The USA, Russia, and western Europe have vast supplies. The world has enough to last for about 200 years. Oil is less common. The world's biggest oilfields are in the Middle East. Saudi Arabia has the largest known reserves.

call the Carboniferous period. Then giant ferns and huge horsetails grew in the warm, swampy forests that covered the land. When the plants died, they became trapped under layers of mud. Over millions of years the mud hardened into rock, and the plant remains changed into layers, or seams, of coal.

Like the plants it came from, coal contains carbon, which gives out plenty of heat when it burns. That is why coal is a good fuel. The best coal, called anthracite, is nearly all carbon. Other coals, like brown coal and bituminous coal, contain less carbon and so produce less heat.

Cutting the coal

Deposits of coal may be found on or near the surface, but are often buried deep underground. Near the surface they are mined by the opencast method. Any covering dirt is stripped away, and power shovels then load the exposed coal into trucks or railway wagons.

When the coal seams lie deep underground, vertical shafts and horizontal tunnels are dug to reach them. The coal is cut from the seams by miners using powerful machines, such as shearers.

POOR PEAT

When vegetable matter gets buried and starts to decay, it forms a black, flaky material called peat. Over millions of years under the right conditions, the peat might turn into coal. Beds of peat are found in many places. Blocks of peat can be dried and used as a low-grade fuel.

◀ **Making their mark**
Fossils of leaves can often be found in coal. These well-preserved examples show the kind of plants that grew in swampy Carboniferous forests.

▼ **The Carboniferous forest**
300 million years ago, warm, steamy forests of giant ferns grew in many parts of the world. It was in such forests that coal was born.

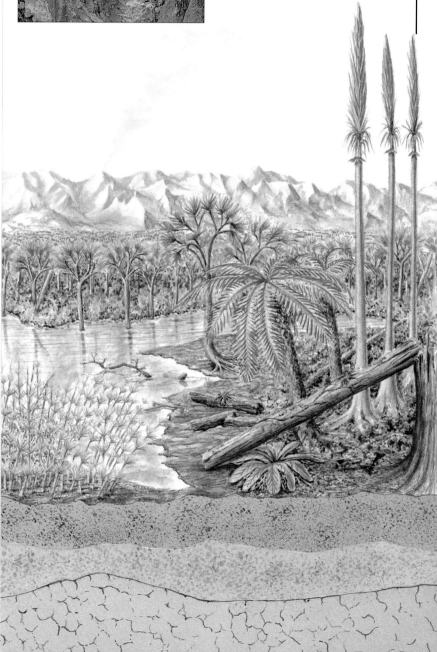

These cutters have rotating heads studded with sharp teeth and can cut as much as 15 tonnes (14 tons) of coal a minute. Conveyors remove the cut coal from the coalface and transport it to hoists that lift it to the surface.

Black and sticky

Oil began forming hundreds of millions of years ago when plant and animal matter decayed into a slimy mess on the seabed and became buried by sand and mud. In time the sand and mud turned to rock and the slimy mess became oil. The oil slowly moved through holes in the rocks until it became trapped.

In places oil seeped up to the surface, where people came across it centuries ago. At first they regarded the sticky black liquid as a nuisance! Then

▼ Pumping by donkey
Pumping machines like this can be seen in most oilfields. They are called 'nodding donkeys' because of their shape and the way they move up and down as they pump.

▲ Oiling a bike
As every child knows, oiling the links of a bicycle chain keeps it running smoothly. Oil oils, or lubricates, moving metal parts by coating them with a thin film. This prevents the metal parts from actually touching each other and causing friction and wear.

NATURAL GAS

When oil was formed long ago, gas was also produced. Often it got trapped in the underground reservoirs where oil is found. However, it is also found by itself.

Like oil, this natural gas is an excellent fuel. It is made up mainly of methane gas, together with heavier gases such as butane and propane. Methane is the gas millions of people use for heating and cooking. The heavier gases are easily liquefied, and they are widely used to provide a portable gas supply, for example, in hot-air balloons.

FROM FIELD TO REFINERY

Oil is often found in remote places, and has to be transported long distances to refineries (right), which will convert it into useful products such as petrol. It may be carried by sea in huge oil tankers, or along pipelines, like the 1,300-km (810-mile) long Trans-Alaskan Pipeline (left).

demand for oil grew as engineers began using it to lubricate their engines and machines, and people started using oil lamps for lighting. By the middle of the nineteenth century, demand had risen so much that people started drilling for oil, and the oil industry was born. First to drill and strike oil was a retired railway worker named Edwin Drake, from Pennsylvania in the United States.

Towering rigs

Today, oil engineers drill for oil all over the world, both on land and under the sea. Some of the biggest oil 'strikes' in recent years have been offshore, for example in the North Sea. To extract this offshore oil, huge rigs have been built, some over 300 metres (985 feet) tall and as big as the Eiffel Tower in Paris.

When oil is brought to the surface, it is known as crude oil or petroleum ('rock oil'). It is a thick, greenish-black liquid, which is not much use as it is. Crude oil only becomes useful when it is refined, or split up into different parts, called fractions. Petrol, kerosene, and diesel oil are just some of the products we get from crude oil.

SPLITTING THE CRUDE

Crude oil is separated into its different fractions in a distillation column called a fractionating tower. Oil vapour passes into the tower, which has many trays maintained at different temperatures. The various fractions condense into liquid in different trays.

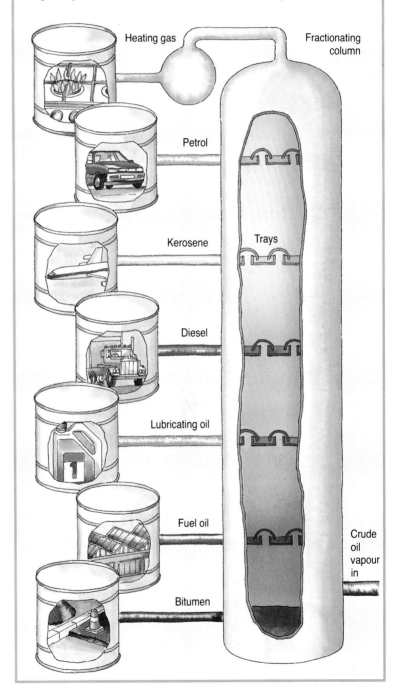

Heating gas

Petrol

Kerosene

Diesel

Lubricating oil

Fuel oil

Bitumen

Fractionating column

Trays

Crude oil vapour in

PETROL AND DIESEL ENGINES

T he most valuable product we get from oil is petrol, which fuels most of our cars. In a petrol engine, the fuel is exploded by an electric spark inside closed cylinders. The gases produced push against pistons, which force round a shaft that connects with the wheels These drive the car. This kind of engine is called an internal combustion engine (ICE). The diesel engine that powers most trucks is another ICE. It is similar, but does not need a spark to ignite its fuel.

We can think of a petrol engine as being made up of a number of different systems, which together make it work. The fuel system supplies petrol to the engine. In many engines petrol is mixed with air in a carburettor to form an explosive mixture, which is then fed to the engine cylinders through valves. In others, fuel is injected into air entering the cylinders.

In the cylinders the fuel mixture is exploded by a spark from the ignition system. This system boosts the low voltage (12 volts) of the car's battery to some 15,000 volts to create the spark.

The lubrication system provides oil to make the moving parts turn smoothly. The cooling system

removes the heat produced when the fuel burns, usually by circulating water through the engine. The hot water then passes through a radiator, where it is cooled by a flow of cool air.

Stroke by stroke

Most car petrol engines have between four and eight cylinders. In each cylinder, a regular sequence, or cycle, of actions takes place which enables the pistons to deliver power. It is called the four-stroke cycle, because actions are repeated after every four piston strokes (movements).

The four stages of the cycle are: Intake – taking fuel mixture into the cylinder, Compression – compressing fuel mixture, Power – forcing the piston down the cylinder, and Exhaust – removing burnt gases.

Two German engineers, Karl Benz and Gottlieb Daimler, developed the first petrol engines in 1885. But these were not very efficient. In 1893 another German engineer, Rudolf Diesel, designed a much more efficient oil engine.

The diesel engine is now widely used to power trucks, buses, and cars, as well as locomotives and ships. Most diesels work on the four-stroke cycle.

▲ Fast and furious

The spectators become a blur as a dragster accelerates down the 400-metre (quarter-mile) track. These fiendish machines often have multiple engines.

▼ Road train

Some of the world's largest trucks can be seen on the dirt roads in the outback of Australia. Most trucks have economical diesel engines.

DIESEL ENGINE

The diesel engine is constructed very much like a petrol engine, but it has no spark plug. Fuel is injected into the air compressed by the second piston stroke and burns because the air is hot. This method is called compression – ignition.

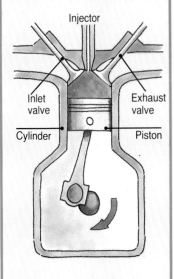

Injector

Inlet valve

Exhaust valve

Cylinder

Piston

STEAM ENGINES

Piston engines driven by steam were the first kinds of engines used in industry and transport. The early ones were great snorting, clanking monsters as big as a house. Later they were more compact and more efficient, and in the 1700s and 1800s they provided the driving force behind the rapid expansion of industry we call the Industrial Revolution. Piston steam engines are not used much today, but steam power lives on in the form of steam turbines. These powerful machines turn generators in the power stations that produce our electricity.

James Watt improved the steam engine out of all recognition in the 1770s. By condensing the steam in a separate cylinder, he made it the first reliable power source for driving machines.

The main parts of a steam engine are a water-filled boiler and a cylinder, in which a piston can move back and forth. A furnace beneath the boiler heats the water into steam. The steam is fed into the cylinder, where it pushes against the piston. The

▲ Going loco
Steam locomotives hauled trains on the railways for more than a century. But today their place has been taken by more efficient, though not so lovable, diesel and electric locomotives.

◄ The power of steam
A miniature steam traction engine burning a few grams of coal puts out enough power to pull a child. This gives an idea of the enormous power steam engines can generate.

34

A GREEK HERO

About 1,900 years ago, a Greek inventor named Hero devised some very interesting machines. One, called the aeolipile (above), was a primitive steam turbine. Steam fed into a sphere escaped through tiny tubes and caused the sphere to spin.

DOUBLE ACTION

In a steam engine, steam is fed into one end of a cylinder, where it produces power by pushing against a piston (top). An ingenious slide valve is used to divert the steam to the other end of the cylinder at the completion of the piston stroke. The steam now forces the piston back again. This is called double-action.

piston moves, and various rods and shafts carry this movement to the machinery to be driven. Valves then switch the steam to the other side of the piston, which is forced back again.

Speedy spinners

The steam turbine works in quite a different way. It consists of a large rotating shaft (rotor) inside a casing (stator). The rotor carries sets of fan-like blades. There are blades on the stator too. Steam from a boiler is fed into the turbine and spins the rotor blades as it rushes through them.

The steam is fed in at high temperature – up to 600°C (1,110°F) – and high pressure – up to 350 kilograms per square centimetre (5,000 pounds per square inch). After passing through the turbine, it enters the condenser. There, it is rapidly cooled and condenses back into water, which is fed back into the boiler. Vast quantities of cooling water circulate through the condenser, as much as 200 million litres (nearly 50 million gallons) every hour!

ALL STEAMED UP

Steam is introduced into a turbine at very high pressure and spins the rotor as it rushes through the turbine blades (below). In a practical turbine, the steam is fed in turn through a number of 'stages', which carry blades of different diameter (above).

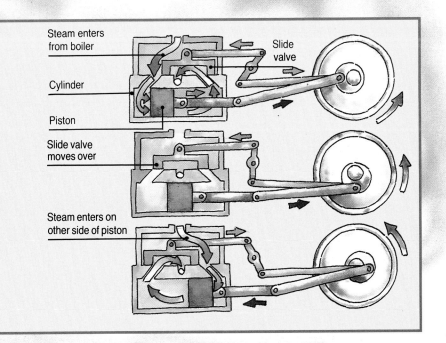

Steam enters from boiler
Slide valve
Cylinder
Piston
Slide valve moves over
Steam enters on other side of piston

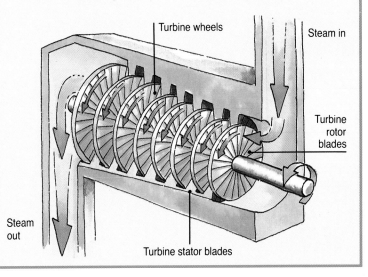

Turbine wheels
Steam in
Turbine rotor blades
Steam out
Turbine stator blades

JET ENGINES

The airliners that whisk us on holiday to distant lands are driven by streams, or jets, of hot gases. Their jet engines burn an oil fuel called kerosene to produce the gases. The force of the gases shooting backwards out of the engines sets up a forward force which drives the plane along. This is the principle of jet propulsion. But aircraft are not the only things that move by jet propulsion. Cuttlefish and squid do, too!

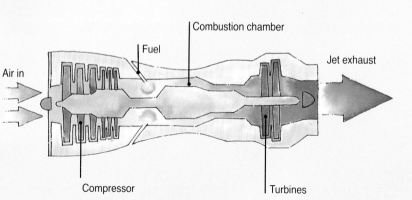

BALLOON JET

If you blow up a balloon and then let it go, it will zoom off, travelling by jet propulsion. The force of the air rushing backwards out of the balloon sets up a similar force forwards, which propels it.

▲ Squirting squid

Squid are sea-dwellers, but they do not swim in the same way as other sea creatures. Instead they travel, backwards, by jet propulsion. They suck water into their bodies and then squirt it out at high speed.

◄ Riding the waves

Among the most exciting modern water sports is jet skiing. Skiers ride a kind of flat-bottomed scooter propelled by water jets. The motor sucks in water and then expels it through nozzles at the rear.

THE JET FAMILY

Three main kinds of jet engine are in common use: the turbojet, turboprop, and turbofan. They are gas-turbine engines, which have one or more turbines spun by hot gas. The British aircraft engineer Frank Whittle patented the gas-turbine engine in 1930.

In a turbojet, all the engine thrust comes from the jet of gases shooting out of the rear nozzle. In a turboprop, the propeller and the escaping jet provide thrust. In a turbofan, the propeller takes the form of an enclosed fan.

TURBOJET

Air in — Compressor — Fuel — Combustion chamber — Turbines — Jet exhaust

Thanks to their jet engines, fighter planes can fly at more than 3,000 km/h (2,000 mph). Many have the simplest type of jet engine, called a turbojet. It consists of a shaft rotating inside a casing. At the front a set of fan-like blades make up the compressor. At the rear a set of blades like a windmill make up the turbine.

The compressor sucks in air and forces it under pressure into a combustion chamber. Fuel is sprayed into the chamber and is ignited and burned. The gases produced spin the blades of the turbine before escaping from a nozzle at the rear of the engine as a jet. The spinning turbine turns the compressor, sucking more air into the engine.

Horses for courses

Most airliners use an engine called a turbofan. It gets its name because it has a huge fan in front of the compressor, which sucks air both into and around the engine. Much of the engine 'thrust' comes from the by-passed air.

Many transport planes, which travel more slowly, are fitted with turboprop engines. These have an extra turbine, which is used to spin a propeller. This provides most of the engine thrust.

▲ Jets in line
Jet airliners wait on the taxiway for clearance to take off. These are tri-jets, with all three engines mounted at the tail end. All modern airliners have turbofan engines.

▶ Propeller jets
Tomorrow's airliners could have propfan engines like this, which uses a fan-like multi-bladed propeller to generate thrust.

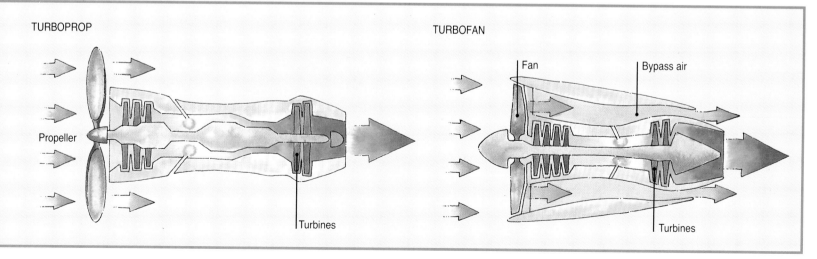

TURBOPROP

Propeller

Turbines

TURBOFAN

Fan

Bypass air

Turbines

ROCKETS

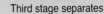 

Third stage separates

Satellite in orbit

Second stage falls away, third stage fires

Second stage fires

First stage falls away

Rockets also work on the principle of jet propulsion. When you light a firework rocket, it sets off a charge of gunpowder. The powder burns and produces a stream of hot gases that drive the rocket up in the air. Space rockets work in a similar way. They can work in space because they carry not only fuel, but also oxygen to burn the fuel.

▶ **Fantastic fireworks**
Rockets carry coloured 'stars' high into the air, where they explode in a kaleidoscope of light. Firework rockets are propelled by a solid propellant, gunpowder. The Chinese invented gunpowder and first used it to make rockets about 800 years ago.

Booster rockets fall away

Booster rockets

Launch gantry

STEP ROCKET

A single rocket cannot develop enough power to lift itself into orbit. All space launch vehicles are made up of several rockets joined together. This arrangement is called a step rocket. Each separate rocket, or stage, fires in turn, then falls away. This allows the next stage to propel the vehicle, now lighter, even faster.

Space rockets need to be powerful because they have to overcome the Earth's pull, or gravity, which is very strong. To get into space, a rocket must reach a speed of at least 28,000 km/h (17,500 mph). This is more than ten times faster than the supersonic airliner Concorde can travel!

At this speed, called orbital velocity, the rocket can travel round and round the Earth in orbit. If it needs to escape from gravity completely, it must travel even faster, at the Earth's escape velocity of 40,000 km/h (25,000 mph).

Solid and liquid rockets

The substances burned to propel a rocket are called

▲ Rockets in the park
A view of the 'rocket park' at Kennedy Space Center, Florida, USA. The author is pictured next to an engine like those used to power the 111-m (365-ft) tall Saturn V Moon rocket. These engines burned kerosene and liquid oxygen as propellants.

LIQUID MOTOR

In a liquid-propellant rocket, fuel and oxidizer are pumped into a combustion chamber where they mix and burn. The hot gases produced develop thrust as they shoot out of the nozzle.

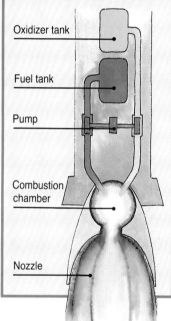

Oxidizer tank

Fuel tank

Pump

Combustion chamber

Nozzle

Nose cone

Satellites

Propellant tanks

Third-stage engine

Oxidizer tank

Fuel tank

Second-stage engine

Oxidizer tank

Fuel tank

Stabilizing fins

First-stage engines

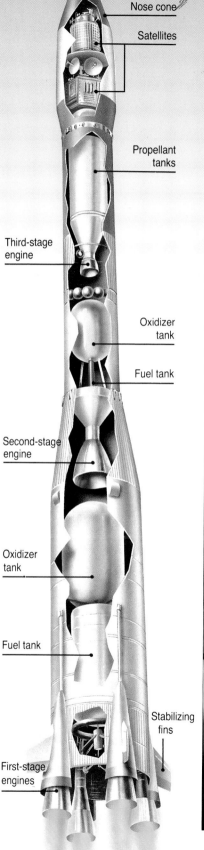

◄ Europe's Ariane
The European Space Agency has developed a family of launch vehicles called Ariane. This one is the basic model. Others have strap-on booster rockets attached. Ariane stands about 50 metres (155 feet) tall and is a three-stage rocket. The five engines of the first stage and the single engine of the second stage have the same propellants. They use a fuel called hydrazine and an oxidizer called nitrogen tetroxide. The single third-stage engine burns liquid hydrogen and liquid oxygen.

▼ America's Delta
A Delta rocket takes off from Cape Canaveral, Florida, USA, carrying a scientific satellite. Solid booster rockets fire to assist lift-off.

propellants. They include a fuel and a substance called an oxidizer, which supplies oxygen to burn the fuel. In some rockets the propellant is solid, and fuel and oxidizer are mixed together. Gunpowder is a propellant like this. Most space rockets have liquid propellants. The fuel and oxidizer are stored in separate tanks and mixed together just before they are burned.

The space shuttle uses both solid and liquid propellant rockets. Its 'strap-on' solid rockets give it extra boost at lift-off. Its three main engines are liquid motors, which burn liquid hydrogen (fuel) and liquid oxygen (oxidizer). This is a powerful, widely used propellant combination.

ENERGY FROM THE ATOM

Everything in the world is made up of basic substances we call the chemical elements. And each element is made up of tiny particles called atoms. The atoms of some elements are unstable, and can be made to split apart. When this happens, enormous energy is given out. We can tap and control this energy and use it to produce electricity and drive nuclear submarines. But atomic energy produces dangerous radiation that can be deadly if it is allowed to escape into the environment.

Most of the mass of an atom is contained in its nucleus, or centre. It is the nucleus that splits and gives out energy. We call the splitting process nuclear fission, and the energy released, nuclear energy.

In nuclear power stations the 'fuel' used to produce energy is a heavy metal called uranium. One kilogram (2.2 pounds) of uranium can produce the same energy as 25 tonnes (24.5 tons) of coal!

In a nuclear power station the fuel is held in the

Neutron

Uranium nucleus

▶ **Chain reaction**
In nuclear fission, a neutron hits and splits a uranium nucleus and two or more neutrons are produced. These split other uranium atoms and this releases still more neutrons. In this way a chain reaction, which produces fantastic energy, builds up.

CERN ATOM-SMASHER

The circle in this aerial picture of Geneva, Switzerland, shows the location of an underground atom-smasher. In it, scientists accelerate beams of atomic particles. They crash the beams into each other to create new particles. The accelerator is operated by CERN, Europe's centre for nuclear research.

UNDER PRESSURE

In a pressurized water reactor, the uranium fuel is packed in rods in the reactor core. Control rods keep the chain reaction going at a safe, steady rate. Water under pressure absorbs the heat produced. It carries hot water to the steam generator, where it is heated into steam. The steam is then fed to turbogenerators which produce electricity.

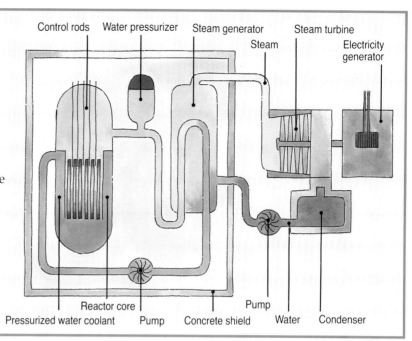

Control rods Water pressurizer Steam generator Steam turbine

Steam Electricity generator

Reactor core Pump

Pressurized water coolant Pump Concrete shield Water Condenser

▲ Beware: Radiation
Radioactive fuel rods must be handled by robot equipment from behind thick protective walls.

▶ Tracking nuclear particles
We can detect nuclear particles by the tracks they leave behind in a detector called a bubble chamber.

core of a vessel called a reactor. A cooling substance, or coolant, circulates through the core and removes the heat given out when the uranium atoms split. It passes into a steam generator, where it boils water into steam. The steam is led away to spin the turbines that turn electricity generators.

Under control

In a reactor the fission process is carefully controlled by means of control rods. They are pulled out or pushed in to make the nuclear reaction go faster or slower. In an emergency they can be pushed right in to shut the reactor down.

The other thing that must be controlled in a nuclear reactor is radiation. Uranium and the products formed in nuclear fission are radioactive, which means that they give off radiation that is harmful to living things. To prevent this radiation from escaping, the reactor is surrounded by a thick wall of reinforced concrete. This is called a biological shield.

SOLAR ENERGY

The Sun bathes the Earth with more energy than we will ever need. People in many places are now harnessing this free energy with solar panels to provide hot water or heat swimming pools. Space satellites harness this energy with solar cells, which turn it into electricity. Solar energy will become more important in the years ahead when the world begins to run out of fossil fuels. We do not have to worry that solar energy will run out: the Sun will carry on shining as it does today for at least another 5,000 million years!

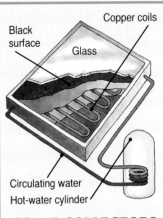

SOLAR COLLECTORS

The wall and roof-top panels used in buildings to trap solar energy are like miniature greenhouses. They are called flat-plate collectors. Solar energy enters through the plate of glass on top and gets trapped inside. Water circulating in coils at the base of the panel extracts the heat and carries it to a hot-water cylinder. The circulating water gives up its heat in the cylinder and then returns to the solar collector.

◄ Sunny side up

This large wall made of hundreds of solar panels is on the south-facing wing of a hospital in Torbay on the south coast of England. Torbay is one of the sunniest places in Britain, and these panels manage to extract plenty of solar heat, even in winter. As in most solar-energy schemes, the heat trapped by the panels is used to heat water for the building's hot-water supply.

Naturally, solar energy is being used most in the sunnier regions of the world. Millions of homes in the south-west United States, around the Mediterranean Sea in Europe and the Middle East, and in Australia are now solar heated. But even in cooler climates, solar power helps reduce fuel bills.

Most solar houses have roof-top collectors in the form of glass-topped panels. They trap the heat of the Sun in the same way that a greenhouse does, and pass the heat to water which is circulating in

pipes. The pipes are connected to the domestic hot-water cylinder, which supplies hot water to the house.

Solar electricity

Different kinds of solar panels can turn solar energy into electricity. Satellites use them to power their instruments. They consist of tiny solar cells made of silicon, the same material used to make computer chips. When sunlight falls on the cells, electrons

▼ Solar power tower

Solar 1, a solar power plant near Barstow in California, USA, produces up to 10 megawatts of electricity – enough to light more than 100,000 light bulbs. The plant consists of some 1,800 mirrors, arranged in circles around the tall central tower, which is 78 metres (256 feet) high. The banks of mirrors reflect sunlight on to a boiler at the top of the tower. Water in the boiler turns to steam, which drives turbogenerators to produce electricity.

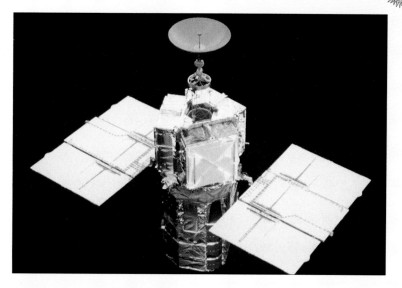

◄ Satellite solar cells

The 'wings' on this satellite carry thousands of tiny solar cells. They each produce a trickle of electricity when sunlight falls on them. Together they generate several thousand watts of electricity to power the satellite's instruments and radio. This satellite, Solar Max, is famous because in April 1964 it was the first satellite to be recovered and repaired. Astronauts spacewalked from the space shuttle *Challenger* to do the work.

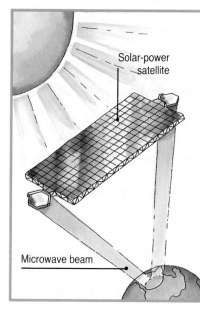

SOLAR ORBITER

Solar-power satellite

Microwave beam

Up in space the Sun always shines, by day and by night, and there are no clouds to block its light. So scientists have suggested building solar power plants in high orbit around the Earth. They would capture solar energy by means of huge panels of solar cells, and then beam it down to Earth in the form of microwaves.

start flowing, setting up an electric current.

Attempts are also being made to produce electricity from sunlight on a commercial scale for feeding into the electricity grid. One scheme is the solar power tower. It uses thousands of mirrors to collect the Sun's rays and reflect them onto a boiler at the top of a central tower. The boiler makes steam to feed electricity generators. The world's largest power-tower scheme, called Solar 1, is located at Barstow in sunny California.

WIND POWER

Our ancestors began harnessing the energy blowing in the wind 5,000 years ago when they rigged up sails on their ships. Sailing ships and wind-powered machines in the form of windmills remained in widespread use until the early twentieth century. Today, wind power is coming back into favour because it is a natural source of energy that will never run out. But traditional windmills have had their day, and are being replaced by highly efficient wind turbines, some of which have very odd shapes.

▼ **Windmills at work**
These windmills, near Zoetermere in the Netherlands, are used for pumping water to drain farmland. Windmills cover the Netherlands. For centuries they were the country's main source of energy, since it had no other natural energy resources, not even water power.

The old type of windmill had large wooden sails and spun round quite slowly. It was designed to turn huge grindstones to mill (grind) grain into flour. Modern wind turbines are designed to spin very much faster. They drive generators that produce electricity.

One of the most common types of wind turbine is found in isolated settlements and farms. It has a turbine wheel, or rotor, consisting of many metal vanes. The most powerful turbines have rotors shaped like propellers. The rotors can be huge. One turbine on the Hawaiian island of Oahu has a rotor that measures more than 120 metres (400 feet) across!

Farming the wind

In some places a group of many small wind turbines rather than a single large one is used to produce electricity. Together they form a 'wind farm'. The largest wind farms can be found in California, in the United States, where they may cover an area of several square kilometres. In the future, wind farms may be sited on artificial islands offshore, where they would pick up the breezes that blow nearly all the time on the coasts.

Some wind farms use a propeller-type turbine, which turns on a horizontal axis, to catch the wind. Others use a peculiar-shaped turbine that looks like an eggbeater. It is called a Darreius turbine after the person who invented it. It turns on a vertical axis, performs well in light winds, and can accept winds from any direction.

▼ Power on the spot
Not so long ago, many isolated farmhouses used wind power to generate their electricity and pump water for their livestock. The circular 'sail' spun in the wind and turned a small turbine to produce power.

▲ Terrible tornado
The enormous energy locked in the wind is demonstrated by the destruction wreaked by tornadoes. A tornado is a funnel-like pocket of wind, spiralling at speeds up to 500 km/h (300 mph) around a region of very low air pressure.

▲ Running with the wind
With their spinnakers (racing sails) set, these yachts run with the wind, harnessing nature's free energy. In skilful hands, yachts can also sail into the wind, by zig-zagging alternately to left and right, a technique called tacking.

THE SOLAR WIND

A 'wind' of sorts blows in space. It is the solar wind, a stream of particles given out by the Sun. Space scientists are looking into the idea of harnessing the power of this wind to drive spacecraft to the planets and beyond. The spacecraft would be fitted with enormous 'sails', which would unfold in space and catch the solar wind.

... and coal – are limited, ... If we continue as we are, ...rs' time. Then we shall ...upplies of coal should last ...tists will have found out ... the stars.

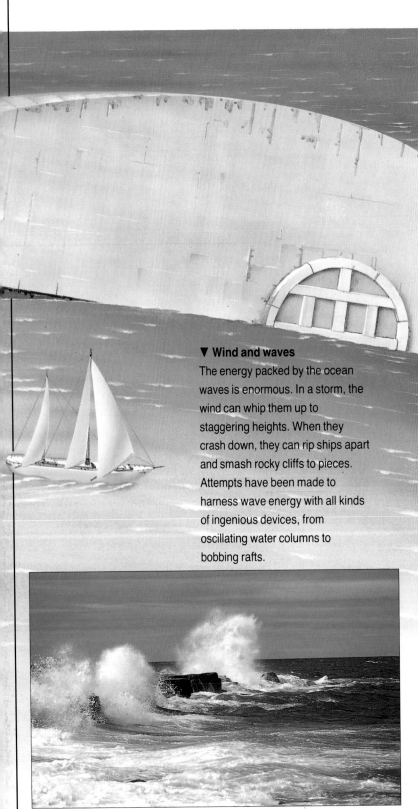

▼ Wind and waves
The energy packed by the ocean waves is enormous. In a storm, the wind can whip them up to staggering heights. When they crash down, they can rip ships apart and smash rocky cliffs to pieces. Attempts have been made to harness wave energy with all kinds of ingenious devices, from oscillating water columns to bobbing rafts.

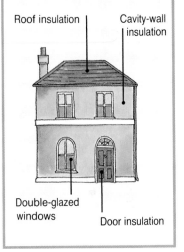

Roof insulation   Cavity-wall insulation

Double-glazed windows   Door insulation

◄ Downtown traffic jam
The streets of our big cities regularly get clogged with traffic. The vehicles waste precious fuel and pour poisonous exhaust fumes into the air. This is causing an increased health hazard.

alternative sources of energy, such as water, wind, and solar power.

Scientists and engineers are helping energy conservation, for example, by designing more efficient, 'lean-burn' engines for our cars. Car engines are by far the biggest consumers of our

RECYCLING WASTE

By recovering and re-using waste materials, we not only save precious resources, but also save the energy needed to process them. Waste paper (left), glass, and aluminium (right) are being successfully recycled. But the cost of collecting waste materials prevents recycling on a much larger scale.

precious oil. Burning less oil is also good for the environment because it reduces pollution.

We can save energy on home heating by insulating our houses better. The more heat we keep in, the less fuel we have to burn. We can save energy by recycling products, or collecting them to be used again. Recycling also saves the energy needed to extract the materials that are used to make the products in the first place.

Energy for ever

Conservation, recycling, and using alternative energy sources will help the world's coming energy problems, but not solve them. Scientists are therefore pinning their hopes on a process of producing energy used by the Sun and the stars (see pages 14–15).

Called nuclear fusion, the process uses for fuel a heavy kind of hydrogen, which can be extracted from the water in the oceans. And the good news is that there is enough of this fuel in the oceans to last us for millions of years!

JET ENERGY

At a laboratory at Culham, England, European scientists are experimenting with nuclear fusion to try to harness the kind of energy that keeps the stars shining. They have built a machine called the Joint European Torus (JET). It is a giant electromagnet with a ring-shaped chamber in the middle. Powerful electric currents and microwaves heat heavy hydrogen atoms in the ring to temperatures up to 300 million degrees Celsius, imitating the conditions in the middle of stars where nuclear fusion takes place. Strong magnetic fields keep the very hot hydrogen fuel (called 'plasma') away from the vessel walls.

ENERGY ESSENTIALS

The world is packed full of energy in a myriad of different forms, from the energy locked up in tiny atoms, to the energy blowing in the wind. By harnessing this energy with engines and turbines, we drive the machines on which our modern world depends. This fact-kit provides you with a summary of essential information about the energy all around us, inside us, and in the Earth beneath us.

1 Before a fall

A ball resting on a table has energy because of its position. We call this kind of energy potential energy. It represents energy stored in a body.

2 On the move

If we nudge the ball so that it falls off the table, it starts moving. The potential energy stored in the ball is converted to the energy of movement, or kinetic energy. Anything that moves has kinetic energy.

3 Turning on the heat

Heat is one of our most familiar forms of energy. It is a property that depends on the movement of the tiny particles of which all matter is made up. Substances get hotter when their particles move faster.

4 Making waves

The Earth receives a great deal of energy from the Sun. The Sun sends out energy as rays, or radiation. These rays take the form of waves. Each one has a different wavelength.

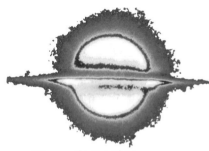

5 Energetic chemistry

We produce most of our energy on Earth by burning fuels. Burning is a chemical process in which fuels combine with the oxygen in the air. Fuels possess chemical energy, locked in the substances from which they are made.

6 Thought for food

Most living things get the energy they need to grow and move about by eating food. Food is the body's fuel. Inside the body the food is 'burned' in oxygen breathed in from the surroundings.

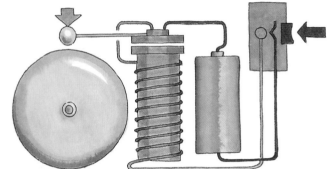

7 Making food with light

Plants can make their own food. Animals cannot. Plants make their food (sugar) by a process called photosynthesis. They make it from water they take in from the soil and carbon dioxide they take in from the air. Sunlight provides the energy to make the process work.

8 Chemical electricity

The energy stored in chemicals can be released as heat (see Item 5). It can also be released in another form – electricity. This is what happens in batteries, like the dry cell.

9 Pressure in wires

Electricity flows in wires when there is electric 'pressure' to make it flow. Batteries supply this 'pressure', which we call voltage. This is

named in honour of the Italian scientist Alessandro Volta, who invented the battery in 1800.

10 Currents in coils

Electricity can also be made to flow in coils of wires when they are spun round near a magnet. This is the principle behind the electric generator. Powerful generators make the 'mains' electricity we use in the home.

11 Fuels from fossils

The fuels we use most – coal, oil, and natural gas – are the remains of plants and animals that lived on the Earth several hundred million years ago. That is why we call them 'fossil fuels'.

12 Old King Coal

Coal was the earliest of the fossil fuels used on a large scale. It was the main fuel used in the world until the middle of this century. In the next century it will almost certainly regain its position as top fuel, when supplies of oil and gas begin to run out.

13 Boring statistics

Oil, or petroleum, is today's most important fuel. It is extracted by boring into the ground. The world produces and uses over 3,000,000 tonnes (3,300,000 tons) of oil a year. The USA and Saudi Arabia are two of the world's biggest producers.

14 How refined

Petroleum is a mixture of hundreds of different chemicals, called hydrocarbons because they contain only hydrogen and carbon. These are separated into a number of parts, or fractions, at an oil refinery.

15 Electric water

Most power stations burn fossil fuels to produce energy to spin the electricity generators. But some power stations harness the energy in flowing water instead. The power they produce is called hydroelectricity.

16 Energetic atoms

There is enormous energy locked up in the nucleus, or centre, of atoms. Scientists have learned how to split the nucleus of some atoms, notably uranium, and release this energy. Nuclear power stations use uranium as 'fuel'.

17 Deadly rays

Weight for weight, uranium 'fuel' can produce hundreds of thousands of times more energy than coal or oil. The problem is that the substances produced when uranium atoms split are highly radioactive. This means that they give off dangerous rays, which are very harmful to living things.

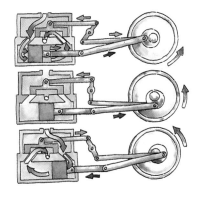

18 At a stroke

Many of our machines are powered by electricity. But mobile machines such as cars are powered by engines, such as petrol and diesel engines. These are piston engines. They burn fuel inside cylinders to make hot gases, and the gases produce power by moving pistons.

19 Terrific turbines

The most powerful engines, however, are not piston engines but turbines. Turbines produce power when steam, water or gases spin their wheel-like blades.

20 Jet-propelled

Aircraft are propelled by gas turbines and work by jet propulsion. These engines burn fuel to produce a stream, or jet, of hot gases. As the gases shoot backwards from the

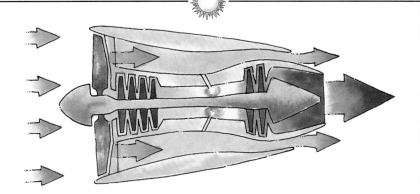

engine, the engine, and thus the aircraft, is thrust forwards.

21 Rocket revelations

Rockets work by jet propulsion too. The difference between a jet and a rocket is that a jet draws in oxygen from the atmosphere, while a rocket carries its own oxygen. That is why a rocket, but not a jet, can work in space.

22 Acid in the rain

Vast quantities of fossil fuels are burned every day. The trouble is that when these fuels burn, they release acid fumes into the atmosphere. When it rains, the raindrops are acid too, and this is harming the environment.

23 Greenhouse in the sky

Burning fuels also release large quantities of carbon dioxide gas into

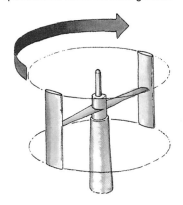

the air. This is getting trapped and gradually building up, turning the atmosphere into a kind of greenhouse. World temperatures are rising as a result.

24 What's the alternative?

One day, when the fossil fuels run out, we shall have to rely on other energy sources. We shall need to extract more of nature's energy, for example, from sunshine, the wind, and the waves.

25 Energy for ever?

In the long term scientists hope to tap the main energy source of the Universe, and imitate the process, nuclear fusion, by which stars produce their energy.

GLOSSARY

(Note: Words in *italics* refer to other entries in the glossary.)

Atoms The smallest particles of something that can exist.

Battery A device that makes electricity by chemical reactions.

Burning What happens when a substance combines with oxygen and gives out light (flame) and heat. A form of oxidation.

Carbohydrates Basic food substances, such as sugar, which the body needs to 'burn' to provide energy.

Carbon dioxide The gas in the air which plants use to make their food.

Celsius scale A scale of *temperature*, on which the freezing point of water is 0 degrees and the boiling point is 100 degrees.

Chain reaction The process that occurs in a nuclear *reactor*, in which more and more *atoms* split and release energy.

Chlorophyll The green pigment in plants that helps food-making take place.

Coal A *fossil fuel* that is the decayed remains of huge tree-like plants that grew hundreds of millions of years ago.

Combustion Another term for *burning*.

Conduction One method by which heat travels in a material. The heat is passed on by the individual particles of which the material is made up.

Conductor A material that passes on heat or electricity well.

Conservation of energy A basic law of science that says, in a closed system, energy can be neither created nor destroyed.

Convection A method by which heat travels in liquids and gases. Heat causes the liquid or gas to expand and rise, setting up a convection current.

Diesel engine An *internal combustion engine* that burns diesel oil for fuel. The *oil* ignites when it is injected into hot compressed air in the cylinders.

Electric current The flow of electrons through a *conductor*, usually a wire.

Electromagnet A temporary *magnet* made by passing electric current through wire coils wound around an iron core. The magnetism ceases when the current is switched off.

Electromagnetic wave A wave consisting of electric and magnetic vibrations. *X-rays, light, ultraviolet,* and *radio waves* are different kinds of electromagnetic waves.

Elements Also called chemical elements. The basic building blocks of matter. More than 90 are found in nature.

Escape velocity The speed at which objects must travel in order to escape completely from the Earth's gravity. It is some 40,000 km/h (25,000 mph).

Fahrenheit scale A *temperature* scale on which water freezes at 32 degrees and boils at 212 degrees.

Fossil fuels Fuels such as *coal, oil,* and *natural gas,* which are the remains of once-living things.

Four-stroke cycle The operating cycle of most *petrol* and *diesel engines,* in which power is produced once in every four strokes (movements) of the pistons.

Gamma rays A kind of *electromagnetic wave* which has very short wavelengths. Gamma rays are very penetrating and can harm living tissue.

Generator A machine that produces electricity.

Geothermal energy Heat extracted from the ground, usually in the form of hot water or steam.

Geyser A kind of hot spring that periodically shoots a jet of steam and hot water into the air.

Greenhouse effect The turning of the atmosphere into a kind of greenhouse, which traps the Sun's heat and increases world temperatures, brought about by increasing amounts of *carbon dioxide* in the air.

Heat One of our most familiar forms of energy. Heat energy is related to the *kinetic energy* possessed by *atoms* and molecules.

Hydroelectric power Electricity produced by harnessing the energy in flowing water.

Infrared rays *Electromagnetic waves* that carry heat energy.

Internal combustion engine (ICE) One in which fuel is burned inside the engine cylinders. *Petrol* and *diesel engines* are internal combustion engines.

Jet engine An engine that is propelled forwards by a stream of gases travelling backwards. It works on the principle of reaction.

Kinetic energy The energy possessed by a body when it is moving.

Light The radiation our eyes are sensitive to. Light rays are kinds of *electromagnetic waves*.

Lightning Streaks of light that travel between the clouds or from clouds to the ground in a thunderstorm. They are discharges of electricity, rather like gigantic electric sparks.

Magnet An object, usually made of iron, which can attract iron and one or two other metals. Its magnetism is concentrated at the ends, known as the poles.

Microwaves *Electromagnetic waves* with a shorter wavelength than *radio waves*.

Natural gas A fuel gas that comes from the ground. It is a *fossil fuel*, formed with *oil* in the rocks.

Nuclear energy Energy extracted from the *nucleus* of *atoms*.

Nuclear fission The splitting of the *nucleus* of an *atom*. It is often accompanied by the release of enormous amounts of energy.

Nuclear fusion The coming together of the nuclei of light *atoms* to create a heavier one. This process is usually accompanied by the release of enormous amounts of energy.

Nucleus The centre of an *atom*, made up mainly of two kinds of atomic particles, protons and neutrons.

Oil A liquid fuel we extract from the ground; properly called *petroleum*.

Orbital velocity The speed a space satellite needs to remain in orbit around the Earth. At a height of about 250 km (150 miles), the orbital velocity is about 28,000 km/h (17,500 mph).

Peat A low-grade fuel, made up of partly decomposed plant remains.

Petrol engine An *internal combustion engine* that burns petrol as fuel. In its cylinders, a mixture of petrol and air is ignited by an electric spark.

Petroleum The correct name for the *oil* we extract from the rocks. The word means 'rock oil'.

Photosynthesis The process by which plants make their food in their green leaves. Sunlight provides the energy for this chemical process in which *carbon dioxide* and water combine to make sugar.

Pollution The poisoning of the environment. The *fossil fuels* in particular cause much pollution, giving off acidic fumes when they burn. *Oil* can cause pollution when it escapes into the sea.

Potential energy The energy a body has by virtue of its position.

Propellant A substance burned to propel a rocket.

Radiation Rays. The most common kind of radiation comes from *electromagnetic waves*, which include *light* rays and *radio waves*. *Radioactive* substances give off dangerous rays, such as *gamma rays*.

Radio waves A form of *electromagnetic wave* with a long wavelength. Radio and TV programmes are broadcast by means of radio waves.

Radioactive Giving off radiation. A few natural *elements* and all the artificial ones are radioactive.

Reactor The part of a nuclear power station in which nuclear reactions take place.

Refinery A chemical plant in which *oil* is split up and processed into useful products.

Rocket An engine propelled by a jet of hot gases. It can work in space because it carries both fuel and the oxygen to burn the fuel.

Solar cell A device made of silicon, which captures the energy in sunlight and turns it into electricity.

Solar energy The energy given out by the Sun.

Steam engine An engine that uses the heat energy in steam. It produces power by making steam force a piston back and forth in a cylinder.

Temperature A measurement of the 'hotness' of a substance: of the kinetic energy of its molecules.

Turbine A machine that produces rotary (turning) motion. It contains a shaft (rotor) carrying sets of wheel-like blades, which turn when a fluid (water, steam, or gas) rushes through them.

Turbofan A kind of *jet engine* which has a huge fan in front.

Turbojet The simplest kind of *jet engine*, in which a jet of hot gases provides all the 'thrust'.

Turboprop A kind of *jet engine* in which part of the 'thrust' comes from a propeller.

Two-stroke cycle An operating cycle for *petrol* and *diesel engines*, in which power is produced once in every two strokes (movements) of the piston.

Ultraviolet rays A kind of *electromagnetic wave* that has a wavelength just shorter than *light* rays. In sunlight, these are the rays that burn you.

Uranium The 'fuel' used in most nuclear reactors. Energy is produced when its *atoms* split.

X-rays A kind of *electromagnetic wave* with a short wavelength, which can pass readily through the body. This enables doctors to take X-ray photographs, for example, of broken bones.

INDEX

(Page numbers in *italics* refer to illustrations and captions.)

O

oceans 51
  currents 48, *48*
  heat 49, *49*
oil 28, *28–9*, 30–1, *30–1*, 50–1
OTEC (ocean thermal energy
  converters) 49
oxygen 17
ozone layer 27, *27*

P

parasites *17*
particles 11, 18, 21, 45
peat 29, *29*
Pelton wheels 47
petrol 10, 31, *31*, 32–3, *32*
photosynthesis 16–17, *16*
plants 16–17, *16*
potential energy *10*, 11, 13, *13*
Proxima Centauri 15

R

radiant energy 12
radiation 21, 26–7, *26–7*
radio waves 12, 26, *26*, 27
radioactivity 40, 41, *41*
recycling 51, *51*
refrigerators 18, 19, *19*
Reykjavik, Iceland 48
rockets 38–9, *38–9*
rocks, geothermal energy 48–9
roller skating *10*

S

satellites *12*, 42, *43*
shock waves *13*
sky-divers 13, *13*
Solar 1 power plant 43, *43*
solar energy *12*, 42–3, *42–3*
solar flares *14*
solar wind *14*, 45, *45*
sound 11
space shuttles 39
spacecraft 38–9, *38–9*, 45, *45*
springs *13*
squid 36, *36*
stars 14–15, 51
static electricity 22
steam power 13, 34–5, *34–5*, 48,
  49
storms 11
Sun 14–15, *14–15*, 18, 21
  energy cycle *12*, 13
  nuclear fusion 14, 15, *15*
  radiation 12, 26–7
  solar energy 42–3, *42–3*
  solar wind *14*, 45, *45*
  sunsets *14*
superconductors 19

T

temperature 19–20
thermometers 19–20, *20*
Thermos flasks 20, *20*
tidal power 46, 47, *47*
torches 23, *23*
tornadoes *45*
tropics 18
turbines
  jet engines 36, *36*, 37
  steam 35, *35*
  water 46, 47, *47*
  wind 44, *45*
turbofans 36, 37, *37*
turbojets 36, *36*, 37
turboprops 36, 37, *37*

U

ultraviolet rays 26, 27, *27*
uranium 40, *40*, *41*

V

Volta, Alessandro 24

W

washing machines 13, *13*
water power 46–7, *46–7*
Watt, James 13, 34
wave energy 48, *48*
waves, electromagnetic 26–7,
  26–7
weather 11, 15, 18
Whittle, Frank 36
wind farms 44, *45*
wind power 44, *44–5*
wind turbines 44, *45*
windmills 44, *44*
winds 11, 21, *21*, 48

X

X-rays *12*, 26, 27, *27*

Y

yachts *45*